LIVING WITH A PARENT
WHO DRINKS TOO MUCH

Judith S. Seixas

Living with a Parent Who drinks Too Much

GREENWILLOW BOOKS
A Division of William Morrow & Company, Inc., New York

Library of Congress Cataloging in Publication Data
Seixas, Judith S   Living with a parent who drinks too much.
Summary: Describes alcoholism, alcoholic behavior, and resulting
family problems. Advises children of alcoholic parents in dealing
with these problems and their own feelings and suggests ways
to make life more bearable and productive.
1. Alcoholism—Juvenile literature. 2. Alcoholics—United States—
Family relationships—Juvenile literature   3. Children of alcoholic
parents—Juvenile literature. [1. Alcoholism. 2. Alcoholics]
I. Title. HV5066.S44   362.8'2   78-11108
ISBN 0-688-80196-X   ISBN 0-688-84196-1 lib. bdg.

For Mark, Meredith, and Laurie,
who lived with Bill

I want to thank each of the following who gave generously of their expertise and skills to help bring this book into being:
Jeanette Bertles, Nikki Dillon, Deborah Link, Ellen Morehouse, Bonnie Nelson, Leslie Parke, Frank Seixas, Elizabeth Shub, Jessica and Danny Smith, and Janet Turner.

Judith S. Seixas

Preface

Many young people who live with an alcoholic parent think, consciously or unconsciously, that somehow they are the cause of their parent's alcoholism. Although it is not in their power to do so, they nevertheless keep trying to "cure" the problem or, at least, do something about it. When the parent's alcoholism continues, they develop feelings of helplessness and hopelessness—feelings that stay with them for the rest of their lives.

This book was written to help children of alcoholics understand what is happening to them and to their parents. It describes alcoholism and identifies the behavior of the alcoholic. It deals with the fact that the parent who keeps on drinking too much is an alcoholic and that alcoholism is an illness. It pinpoints the inevitable struggles that arise within family relationships.

Young people who are caught in the web of adult alcoholism tend to react, rather than act, to change their situation. They usually have no idea that it is possible for them to be in charge of their lives while coping with what is going on at home. Many of them are unaware of the problems of the "other" or nonalcoholic parent. Few of them know that as adults they themselves will be at a high risk to become alcoholic. Few of them know where to turn for help.

Living with a Parent Who Drinks Too Much offers no false promises. Instead, it shows how others have dealt with similar problems and feelings. It suggests specific things that can be done to make life more bearable and more productive. And it tells where help is available.

Contents

1
Amy

Amy made a nest for herself in her room. She put a big sign on the door: "Knock Before You Enter!" She had a fuzzy cover on her bed. Sometimes, instead of making her bed in the morning, she would shape the sheets and blankets into a nestlike circle which would be exactly the right size for her to curl up in. Often she moved the bed near the window so that she could lie on it and look at the sky and the branch of a tree that went across the window. Only the branch interrupted her clear view of the weather. There were times when she really felt like a bird.

To get out of the nest, she would place her pillow on the floor to make a soft step down to a shag rug. It kept her feet warm. On a small table next to her bed she kept some special things: a tiny wooden mouse, painted white with pink ears; a square box in which she kept the silver chain she had gotten as a Christmas present from her father; and a supply of peanuts and M&Ms. There was also her favorite book, *Goodnight Moon,* always within reach. She had had the book since she was a very little girl, but it was still her favorite. Nearby she also kept a collection of bright postcards, which her uncle had sent from his trips around the world. Some she taped to the walls.

Today, as an adult, when Amy talks about her room, she says how good it felt to be in it—how much she loved its coziness, the familiar objects, and the bright colors of the postcards. She also talks about her room as a place to which she could escape when the going got tough in her family. Her mother drank too much. Amy's way of handling the situation was to have a place of her own to go where she couldn't hear what was happening in the rest of the house. One thing she could usually be sure of: that her mother was so busy with her own problem that she wouldn't even miss Amy.

From the time she was very young, Amy felt uneasy about her family; she knew there was something about them that separated them from others. At first she didn't know exactly what the problem was. The *Dick and Jane* books that she read in school brought clearly to her attention that her family was different from others. She couldn't believe that families lived the way Dick and Jane's family lived, had orderly meals, clean dogs, and peaceful households. Yet she felt uncomfortable about her family, and she continued to wonder why. At about the same time, during visits to neighbors, she saw that other families did, in fact, behave differently from hers. Although Amy felt sure that most of the time her mother was like other mothers and she loved her very much, she began to hide what was going on at home. She didn't want the outside world to know. Most of the time she didn't mind how she was treated at home as long as outsiders didn't find out about it. She was ashamed of everything and everyone, including her three younger sisters, and she began to worry about bringing friends to the house.

In a family like Amy's, where a mother, a father, or both parents drink too much, problems are always springing up. It is hard to know what to expect. Some days may be peaceful; other days and nights may be disasters. Amy managed to get away from the fighting by going to her room and shutting the door. But even when she was physically away from the quarreling, she couldn't help worrying about what was going on. When she was out of the house, she would wonder what might be happening there. Amy tried not to think about the troubles at home, but the feelings of terror and loneliness stayed with her.

In this book you will learn that many of your feelings are much the same as Amy's and that many young people live in families such as yours. Like Amy, you may feel lonely, but you are not alone. There are lots of children in this country, in your town, and probably even on your street who live with a parent who drinks too much. It is estimated that in the United States twenty million children live with at least one parent with a serious drinking problem.

As you already know, your parent who drinks too much makes life difficult, not only for himself or herself, but for you and your family. The ways in which you are affected partly depend on whether it is your mother or your father who drinks too much. It may also depend on whether you are a boy or a girl. In most of this book you will find the drinking parent referred to as "he," and "he" is used instead of "he/she" or "him/her." But that doesn't mean that the parent who drinks too much is always a father; just as often it is a mother. Of course, to make sense out of what you read, you will have to relate it to the person in your home who has the drinking problem.

Reading this book and finding that others have felt, or feel now, the way you do may not help you enough. And just being told that you are not alone and that your family's troubles are not your fault will not solve your problem. This book will encourage you to find out what help is available to you. Chapter V includes references to people and agencies that are concerned about children with problems such as yours. It will take effort and courage on your part to find such help, but it will be well worth it. Blaming yourself or bearing the brunt of your parent's difficulties is useless. It is not your fault; you didn't cause the problem, nor can you solve it alone.

Alcoholism is a disease, one that is difficult to understand. In this book you will learn more about it. Why does a person drink too much? Why did this happen to your parent? What does the drinking have to do with you? How can you help your parent with a drinking problem? And how can you help yourself?

Most of the stories in this book are based on

real-life histories. Some are taken from the reports of therapists who are treating children and adults who are still living with or who have lived with a drinking family member. Others are excerpts from letters that adults have written about their childhood. All these adults grew up in homes similar to yours and are now able to tell about their childhood experiences, how they suffered and how they managed. Amy is one of them.

2
Alcoholism–
Your Parent Who
Drinks Too Much

It took Amy a long time to realize that her mother was an alcoholic. When she finally did, she felt relieved. Until then she had blamed her parents' actions on herself. Now she knew that their unexplained and, to her, sometimes mysterious behavior was related to her mother's drinking. She was at last aware that she couldn't do much about it, that she was not to blame for it, and that she would have to find ways of living with and accepting the situation. For many months she had to keep reminding herself that her mother was an alcoholic. She even wrote a note to herself which said, "My mother is an alcoholic. She is sick." She kept it inside the cover of the book on the table next to her "nest."

You probably wonder why people lose control of their drinking and become alcoholics. It is a complicated subject and one that still needs a lot of study. It is known that alcohol is a drug that makes most people feel relaxed and generally good. However, there are people who react differently; it makes them feel uneasy. There are people who feel so sick to their stomachs and dizzy the first time they take a drink they decide never to try it again. In other words, people react in different ways to this drug. The person who becomes addicted to alcohol is one who finds, at least at the beginning, that it works for him. It makes him feel better, helps him forget troubles, and makes the world look like a happier place. If he is shy or lonely or tense or disappointed, an alcoholic drink makes the uncomfortable feeling go away. Painful feelings can be covered up by drinking, and often problems *seem* to be solved. Most people do not lose control of their drinking.

They realize that the alcohol which may make them feel friendly, funny, sexy, and able to do things they couldn't ordinarily do doesn't offer any permanent solutions. They know that eventually they are going to have to face their personal problems and solve them. Alcohol will not do it for them.

You probably know many people who take a drink in the evenings before dinner or drink wine with their meals or drink when they are at parties. If they don't lose control of their drinking and stop after one or two, they do not have alcoholism. They are "social drinkers." Drinking for them continues to be a pleasant custom and seldom leads to drunkenness.

The way in which a drink affects a person depends on his weight, how much food is in his stomach, how fast he drinks, how accustomed he is to drinking, and possibly some built-in biological and genetic factors. The person who has had too much to drink has trouble talking and trouble walking, his coordination is affected, his reactions are slowed down, and his ability to think clearly is impaired. Something changes in how his mind and body work together. You probably recognize these changes in your parent when he has been drinking.

The person who becomes alcoholic loses control over his drinking, and the time comes when his body *must* have alcohol in order to function. He has become "hooked." He can't give up drinking even when he really wants to. He begins to need more and more alcohol to get the "high" that he is looking for. This is called tolerance. It is a part of any kind of drug addiction. A person who drinks too much will need more and more alcohol to get the same effect and will feel sick if he does not get it.

Once a person has developed tolerance and also must have alcohol to control shaking and other withdrawal symptoms, you know that he is physiologically addicted and that he is an alcoholic. He will also change physically as time goes on.

One boy, Danny, has a father who drinks nothing but beer. He drinks all afternoon on Saturdays and Sundays, and he drinks every evening until he falls asleep. As he drinks, he watches sports on TV. He looks at football or baseball, and sometimes he just turns on the television in order to have an excuse to drink. Danny's father used to be strong and lean; now he has a flabby stomach, and his arms and legs are skinny. His face is puffy and reddish. Because the change was gradual, it went unnoticed by the family. But Danny's aunt, who hadn't seen her brother for two years, remarked on it, and this brought it abruptly to everyone's attention. Danny was shocked and unhappy when he realized how his active father had turned into a lump who did nothing but sit in front of TV smoking cigarettes and drinking beer.

Not all alcoholics are addicted physiologically at first. Many begin by using alcohol to solve problems, and the time when they *must* have it comes years later. You may not even have been born at the time when your mother or father started to drink and discovered that alcohol seemed like a way of easing problems. Most people first drink in junior high school or high school or soon after they graduate. They usually know little about alcohol and how it affects the mind and body. They simply find that alcohol makes them feel good and makes them relaxed and friendly. They may start to drink because they see friends drinking and want to try it. Other people start to drink because they see their parents drinking and they connect drinking with being grown-up.

For your alcoholic parent it probably became harder and harder to deal with unhappiness or problems or decision-making without drinking. Now he or she must have alcohol a lot of the time. A person who cannot give up drinking even when he wants to is an alcoholic, and he is sick. He drinks differently from the person who drinks in moderation. For example:

- He may gulp his drinks.
- He probably can drink a lot before
  he gets drunk.
- He may stay drunk for several days.
- He probably has a favorite drink, like
  beer or scotch.
- He may change from one favorite drink to

another. It may be wine one week and vodka and tonic the next. (This may also mean that he is trying to control his drinking.)

- He may try to hide his drinking.
- He may hide bottles in closets, under pillows, in the basement, in little-used kitchen cabinets, in the car trunk, or—the back of a toilet. Alcoholics are ingenious at finding hiding places.
- He may talk a lot about drinking, drinks, and drunks.
- He may choose friends who also drink too much.
- He may always insist on eating in places where he can have an alcoholic drink with his meal.
- He may not eat much at all. He may drink instead.
- He may sleep a lot, or he may sleep at times when most people are awake. He may get up in the middle of the night.

- He may have blackouts. Someone in an alcoholic blackout continues to function but simply doesn't remember what went on during the time of memory loss. He may forget a little incident or a whole evening or day. He may forget an important event or a phone call. He may forget that he said something to you and will repeat it all over again. Blackouts are an early symptom of alcoholism. We don't know exactly what happens to cause time periods to be forgotten, but we know alcohol affects the neurological functioning of the brain.

- He may have shakes or trembles. The shaking that you see is most often in the hands or around the mouth and jaw. It occurs when the body, which has become used to having alcohol, is not getting what it needs. At such a time the alcoholic may have trouble holding a cup of coffee or orange juice, or he may cut himself if he tries to shave. The person who

has the shakes is usually embarrassed by
them. So he may drink in the morning
to stop the shaking. This remedy is only
temporary. When the effects of the drink
start to wear off, the shaking comes back.

Alcoholism is an illness. The person with alcoholism is sick. He feels awful most of the
time. His mind is fuzzy. He gets sicker and sicker
until he decides to make a change and stop drinking. You can't make that decision for him; he
has to make it for himself. Alcoholism is an illness
that cannot be controlled through willpower alone.
It is an illness which usually requires medical and
psychiatric treatment before the sick person can
get well. The sooner the treatment begins, the
better the chances of recovery. Unfortunately, it
takes a long time for some alcoholics to realize
what they are doing to themselves and to the people around them, and they continue to drink.

STOPPING

Why can't the alcoholic just stop? You can stop eating when you feel full. You can stop running when you are out of breath. So why can't the alcoholic person stop drinking when it can cause so much trouble? One reason he continues to drink is that he is afraid to stop; he knows how awful he feels when he does not drink.

The time may come when your parent who has been drinking too much may become so sick and tired of being sick and tired that he will decide to try to stop drinking. He may not be doing his work well anymore, although he often doesn't realize it. He may be in trouble with his boss, who will probably talk to him about his drinking. Or he may be talked to about the quality of his work. He may have lost his driver's license, or he may have hurt someone or smashed his car. He may have trouble sleeping or eating or getting up in the morning. He may be having too many miserable times with his family and friends. His health may be seriously affected. Before it happens, it is just about impossible to know what will make a person want to try to stop drinking.

Perhaps your mother or father has stopped or tried to stop drinking many times. Certainly there are things that you have tried to do and have not been able to do the first time you tried. Do you remember learning to ride a bike? It took time. You may have had trouble learning, but you didn't give up. It just meant that you had to try harder, and eventually you learned. It is a hopeful sign when someone keeps trying. You know that he knows that there is a problem, and you know that he is trying to help himself.

DETOXIFICATION

People who stop drinking sometimes have to go to the hospital or a special facility to be detoxified, or "dried out." The hospital is the best place for treatment.

The entire body must adjust to a new chemical makeup, and the withdrawal symptoms (such as sweating, fever, pains, nausea, and shakes) can be severe and dangerous. The use of carefully controlled drugs to calm the person, and the help of doctors and nurses, will make the withdrawal less difficult and minimize the suffering. This process usually takes several days. One thing you can be sure of: After the alcohol is out of the patient's body, the sick person will look and feel a lot better.

REHABILITATION

After detoxification there will be a period of rehabilitation during which the alcoholic person starts to recover both physically and mentally. To get back to normal health usually takes weeks and sometimes months. This really isn't surprising since he has probably been drinking for years.

You will be living with a parent who is having to make adjustments that will affect everyone in the family. There is a good chance that he will be going to Alcoholics Anonymous meetings. These meetings are made up of groups of recovering alcoholics who get together to help one another stay sober. The parent who is beginning a new life needs these meetings. He may need to attend them as often as every night. Sometimes a family will feel deserted when they see that the alcoholic has finally gotten better and then spends so much time going out to AA meetings. The family must realize that these meetings are helping him stay sober; certainly that is what they want! At the same time it's annoying that he must be gone so much because after all, that was one of the problems while he was drinking. As time goes on, he will not need to attend as many meetings; he may always need some.

You undoubtedly have noticed, too, that he spends lots of time on the telephone and that this actually takes him away from you. You have a right to feel annoyed and jealous that your parent has become so involved with AA friends. After a while you can tell him how you feel about that, and you can tell him that his new friends seem more important to him than you. Maybe together you can work out a balance so that he will spend time with you and still have enough energy to devote to AA people and meetings. Making these new adjustments is a task for the whole family.

Your parent must learn a new way to use the time he spent drinking. He must find his place again in the family. Family members have learned from experience not to trust him. He has been acting irresponsibly for a long time. In addition to doing things with you, he will have to find other things to do that interest him. Most important, he is going to have to deal with his unhappiness and disappointment about himself without resorting to drinking. If he gets angry or feels down, he cannot now use drinking as a way of handling these feelings. During rehabilitation he has started to learn how to live with some discomfort. But as he continues to experience these feelings, he must learn healthy ways to cope with them.

Because a recovering alcoholic is embarrassed about what went on during the time he was drinking, he usually tells his family not to talk about it, or about the struggles involved in staying sober. It may be confusing when he himself talks freely to friends and neighbors about how well he feels now that he is no longer drinking. You can respect the fact that he wants to be the one to break the news to people outside the family. If there is talk about his recovery, he wants to be the one to do it.

You can be helpful to him through the recovery period. Try to avoid unnecessary arguments, and try to keep the household running as smoothly as possible. Try to show him love and faith, and let him know that you are happy about the fact that he is no longer drinking too much.

When a parent stops drinking, the reorganization of the family affects everyone. One boy ate spaghetti out of a can for every meal while his mother was drinking. She didn't have the energy to prepare anything more elaborate for him. She spent most of the time in bed. When she stopped drinking and took command of the kitchen, her son had to eat what was prepared for him. Even though he felt good about the fact that his mother was better, he nevertheless had become used to eating what, when, and where he chose. He felt grown-up getting his own meals. Now he was angry that his mother didn't trust him and insisted on doing all the cooking herself.

Another boy had taken over the care of his two-year-old brother while his mother had been drinking. He developed a very special relationship with his brother, and he enjoyed taking him around the neighborhood. When his mother stopped drinking, she insisted on taking care of the little boy herself, and she refused to let the older boy take him out any longer. The boy resented this, and he also missed the proud, warm feelings he had had while caring for his brother. It seemed as if his mother was spoiling everything.

Another common experience for children who live with recovering alcoholics is "overdisciplining." The parents interfere in situations where the children feel they have no business. One girl told about her mother who, when she had been drinking, hadn't cared when her daughter came home from school. Now that the mother was sober she insisted that the girl be home at three o'clock.

This was much earlier than her friends had to be in. The girl was furious that her mother had set up a new rule, especially since she had been free to come and go as she pleased.

However, a friend of her mother's suggested that she wait until her mother had been sober for a longer period as that would be a better time to discuss more flexible hours. Obviously, when the girl had basketball practice after school or wanted to go to a friend's house, she couldn't be home at three o'clock, and there was no reason why she should be. Her mother, on the other hand, was trying to make up for the time when everything had been out of control and was asking her family to do a lot of things that seemed unreasonable and unnecessary. Yet what she needed from her children were explanations and reassurance. You may find that in ways you become the mother to your mother. In time this will undoubtedly change, and the relationships among family members will become more normal. The children will be cared for, and the grown-ups will again take on the responsibilities which are theirs. They will no longer overreact and be overanxious and strict. The strictness is related to guilt about what they did *not* do when they were drinking.

As your parent gets better, you will notice that your family has had to rearrange itself. Your family may suddenly seem unfamiliar to you. You can try to make this new family a happier one.

SETBACKS

You can also be helpful if your parent goes back to drinking. Setbacks or slips are common. They happen in most illnesses. Even though you will be disappointed, try not to be critical. A time will come when your parent will again make the effort to stop drinking. Remember your parent is struggling and changing. You can feel encouraged about that. This is the time to be patient and understanding and to realize that problems that took years to develop cannot be solved in a short time. And at least you know that your sick parent has taken a step toward getting better.

3
Life with Your Family

Your life is different from the lives of children who live in homes where no one drinks too much. When you visit the households of friends or relatives, you may see the difference. Amy first realized the difference when she read the *Dick and Jane* books. Your parents may be loving and kind, and there are other ways in which your household may be much like those of your friends. But at the same time there are things going on in your house that are typical of families in which someone is alcoholic. You live with people who behave in ways that are related to their drinking, and you will probably recognize many of the behavior patterns that are discussed here.

EXPECTING THE UNEXPECTED

The alcoholic is unpredictable. You may not know what to expect from day to day or, for that matter, from minute to minute. And since the other family members must react to the alcoholic's moods, they too become unpredictable. You may expect your drinking parent to be angry about something, and surprisingly he or she may not even notice it. Or you may think that things are straightening out, and all of a sudden things are as confused as ever. It may be impossible for you to keep up with your parent's changing view of what is right and what is wrong. One day you may be scolded for not coming home directly after school; the next day you may stay out late and no one will say anything.

Kids of alcoholic parents learn to live "one day at a time" and accept the fact that plans, rules, and feelings all change without reason and without warning.

Since this is your home, most of the time you

can't get away from what is going on there. You are in the middle of it. In addition, even when you are out of the house, you probably can't help worrying about things at home. And you certainly can't predict what it's going to be like when you step inside the door. If you can learn to "let go" of your parent's problem when you are out of the house, you will feel freer to concentrate on your own life, and friends, and fun.

FIGHTING

Almost every kid with an alcoholic in his home describes the awful fighting and arguing that goes on. They all talk about the shouting and yelling between their parents, which often involves them as well. They claim that cursing and swearing are so common that after a while no one notices them. Only when an outsider comes into the house do people watch their language. They talk, too, about the physical brutality and rough treatment that family members inflict on one another. Amy will never forget the time her mother kicked her father so hard that he limped for a week. Once in a while a kid is beaten up by a drinking parent.

The fights are frightening for everyone; no one knows what is going to happen. Anyone might become the target for a blow. The alcoholic, after starting a battle, is likely to walk out or fall asleep, leaving the stunned family to pick up the pieces.

NOISE

When there is so much fighting in a household, it becomes a noisy place in which to live. The shouting and crying will keep the family awake at night. When no one gets enough sleep, tempers grow short, and that leads to more illogical fights. As you know, Amy managed to cut out her parents' arguments by shutting the door to her "nest" or by going out and spending as little time at home as possible. She said that once her mother started talking, she never stopped. She would go on and on, saying the same things over and over again. Most of the time she wasn't even conscious of repeating herself. There are usually ways to get away from the racket. You will find the one that is best for you.

PROMISES AND DISAPPOINTMENTS

Most kids who live in a household with an alcoholic parent know what it means to have promises broken. Jessie, an eleven-year-old girl, went for a drive with her father. She loved her father and loved spending time with him. Soon after they started, he stopped the car and told her to wait for him. He promised he would be back soon. He went into a bar and got so involved with his drinking and friends that he forgot about Jessie. It was a long time before he came out. Jessie felt so hurt she couldn't even talk to him on the ride home. Her anger and helplessness overpowered her. That night she cried for a long time. The next day her father gave her a candy bar. He was trying to make up for Jessie's fear and disappointment. He was also bribing her not to talk about what had happened. Jessie would much rather have had a hug and some loving attention than a candy bar. She came to realize that promises and presents go together. She knew that the present was an attempt by her father to win back her love when he was feeling guilty about having broken his promise.

It was not until many years later that Jessie could talk about this incident and express her fury at her father.

Danny's beer-drinking father promised to take him to a ball game, but he didn't show up. Danny was understandably angry. It was hard for him to believe that his father had meant to go to the game at all. Danny began to lose faith in his father because of the father's outright meanness. Actually, Danny's father had not consciously changed his mind, nor was he uncaring of his son. Like many people who drink too much, he had become preoccupied by the drinking and simply forgot his promise. When you live with a parent with a drinking problem, be prepared for disappointments; they will inevitably happen.

MISUNDERSTANDINGS

In all homes there are misunderstandings between parents and children. However, the difficulties in communicating with one another become even more complicated in a family where there is a person or persons who drink too much.

Family members often don't pay attention to what is said because they are involved with their own thoughts. In some families kids are so accustomed to getting nasty reactions that they are afraid to ask questions or to express opinions. Have you ever been afraid to ask your mother if you could stay up late to watch TV because she might fly into a rage? Or to ask your father for your allowance because he might jump down your throat? When people are upset, they don't really listen to one another. They fly off the handle easily and unexpectedly.

The alcoholic sometimes doesn't remember even when he does hear. Jessie's father yelled at her because he *thought* she hadn't come from school at three, which was the hour that she was supposed to be home. Actually, she *was* home at three. She said, "Daddy, it seems to you that I wasn't home at three, but I really was. I guess I can't prove it to you, but I was at home. Anyway, I'm sorry you're upset." Luckily Jessie realized that her father had been drinking and really had not known whether she was home or not. It was easier for her to accept his unfairness because she knew he was not himself.

UPS AND DOWNS

Ups and downs are common in families in which there is an alcoholic. One moment your parent may be short-tempered and weepy, and the next he may be happy and jolly.

When Amy tells about her mother, she says, "One day Mom would want me to stay with her all afternoon. She would say she didn't know if I loved her . . . and I could prove that I loved her if I would just stay home. The very next day she would be horrid and tell me that I was spending too much time at home. I was really confused and messed up. I didn't know whether my mother wanted me home or not, and I didn't know if she loved me or not." When such changes of mood occur in a parent at the whim of a moment, everyone in the family feels troubled and insecure.

CONFUSION AND FILTH

There are situations in which the alcoholic, struggling to act "normal" and deny that he is sick, will be overly neat and clean and try desperately to keep his life and home in order. He may overdress and spend an amazing amount of time keeping himself clean. But in most cases he will eventually fail in his attempt to keep things together. Then his home will become messy and uncared for. He will begin to neglect himself as well. And as the household becomes more and more disorganized, belongings are lost or misplaced.

Amy described the kitchen in her home: "There were always dirty dishes in and around the sink, food on the floor, and cockroaches having free meals." She was totally disgusted with her home and much too embarrassed to bring her friends there. She blamed the confusion and filth on her mother. She knew that broken things were never repaired. The bathroom had not had a light for months. She believed everyone in the family, including her sisters, was selfish and careless. She complained that her mother was never on time for appointments and sometimes didn't show up at all. She was so embarrassed by her mother's un-reliability that she tried to avoid having to meet her or make any commitments that involved her. She dropped out of the Girl Scouts when the troop planned a mother/daughter dinner.

Everything in the house seemed to get lost or misplaced. One of her sisters had lost the keys to the front door, so Amy couldn't get in unless someone was at home. Many times, when she came home, her mother was there, but drunk, in bed, and didn't hear the doorbell. Each day, when she had to leave her "nest," she prayed for help with the small practical problems of living which are automatically taken care of for most kids.

EMBARRASSMENTS

Embarrassments are common in homes where someone is drinking too much. Understandably, kids never get used to them. You are more sensitive to such situations if you are the kind of person who takes responsibility for what other people do. If your parents are drunk, you may take it personally, and you feel awful for them. You may be ashamed about what other people think. Your parents are the ones that should feel upset about their actions, not you!

Most of the embarrassments have to do with social situations. Drunk people act in ways that are totally unacceptable in our society, and their actions are embarrassing. Being overly friendly and sexy is embarrassing; being sloppy or half-dressed is embarrassing; being bleary-eyed and wobbly in the middle of the afternoon is embarrassing; sleeping on the living-room floor is embarrassing; fights between your parents are embarrassing; overdoing kindnesses and giving extra presents are embarrassing; yelling at strangers is embarrassing. It is a list that can go on and on.

If your mother is drinking too much, she may say silly, inappropriate things that have nothing to do with what is going on. She may spill food as she is putting it on the table. Or she may wear dirty or torn clothing. She may wear a raincoat every day instead of getting dressed. She may forget an appointment at school, and if she does get there, she may have forgotten to comb her hair and button her clothing. Amy was embarrassed one year when her parents didn't come to see her in a school play. But it wasn't half as embarrassing as the next year when her mother came drunk.

If it is your father who is drinking too much, he also may crack jokes that are not funny, but just embarrassing. He may be horrible to your friends, and he may be mean to you in front of them. At times he will say or do things that are completely crazy or unexpected.

Many kids with alcoholic parents are not taken care of. It is painful to realize that your friends get much more help with their daily lives—meals, laundry, homework, social plans—than you do. Amy tells another story about how she went to school on a cold, rainy November day in her shorts and sneakers. She nearly froze on her way, and when she got there, she realized, much too late, that she had made a terrible mistake. All the kids in her class were dressed in warm pants and sweaters. Her classmates thought it was funny to see someone in shorts on such a cold day; her teacher sent her to the nurse's office, where she was given dry clothing. Her mother had been asleep when she left home, and there was no one to help her find the right clothing. She hadn't dared awaken her mother before school because she knew, from experience, that getting her up early would mean a horrible screaming scene. Not only did Amy feel embarrassed, but she also felt unprotected by her mother. She felt that her mother was not taking care of her, and it made her afraid. She needed help that she deserved and wasn't getting.

MONEY

Lack of money often accompanies alcoholism. A person who drinks too much often loses a job or makes less money than his skills and training warrant. In addition, funds are spent on liquor or beer. Drinking is expensive; drinking in taverns or bars is even more expensive. What's more, poor money management plagues the families of most people who drink too much.

Mrs. Miller drinks too much. She lost her part-time job because the drinking affected her work. The money she made had covered the cost of some family luxuries. The Millers' TV set was broken, but there was no extra money to have it repaired. No one needs a television set, but everyone would like to have one. The family was touchy and angry. The result was fighting, arguing, and confusion about things that had nothing to do with the broken TV.

The Millers had four children. The younger children played and made noise. They disturbed the two older ones, who wanted to do their home-work. An argument started. This infuriated Mr. Miller, who wanted peace in the evenings. Mrs. Miller was unable to get dinner ready on time. More arguments started up about who should help her. She also found it difficult to clean the house or put things away. Belongings were lost. Her drinking sapped her energy. Again, this disappointed her husband, and he got more upset. At the same time he felt that he was the cause of her drinking. Mrs. Miller, in turn, became even more discouraged and spent more time drinking and sleeping. She was getting sicker. The family seemed to be on a merry-go-round they couldn't get off. They took out their frustrations and unhappiness on one another.

More money, of course, would not have helped Mrs. Miller get well. However, it might have reduced the number of problems in the household.

If you would like to have money to spend on yourself, why not earn some? Do you know how to look for a job? Do you know what other kids do to make spending money? Many schools help kids get work through their guidance departments. It was Danny who told how he and his friend, Mark, decided to make money to buy things for themselves. Danny wanted enough money to buy ice cream after school, and Mark wanted comic books, which his parents refused to buy for him. So the boys decided to work together as a cleanup team. On Saturdays they went from house to house, asking for odd jobs. They were asked to do lots of routine things, such as dog walking, window cleaning, and leaf raking. Once they were asked to take care of a man's turtle when he went on a business trip. Because Mark and Danny liked working together, the jobs were fun, and their Saturdays flew by.

If your family is short on funds, anything you can do to earn your own spending money will be helpful. You will feed good about yourself, knowing that you can earn money when you want to.

A PLAN FOR YOUR FAMILY

A person who drinks too much is often forgetful. But sometimes he pretends to remember. The result is always confusion. By writing things down, everyone can be reminded about exactly what decisions have been made. Perhaps you and your parents can sit down together when neither of them has been drinking and write out some rules for the entire family. Then, when problems arise, having things in writing may help avoid misunder-standings. It is a good idea, for example, to make a list assigning household chores:

Who is expected to help with household cleanup tasks?

Does everyone make his own bed?

Who is expected to help with meal planning, cooking, table setting, kitchen cleanup?

Who shops for the groceries?

Who takes out the garbage?

Who takes care of any pets you may have?

Who answers the phone?

Who does the laundry? Who puts it away?

Who empties wastepaper baskets?

Who puts the bikes away or sees if anything is left outdoors?

What is the system for cleaning your home? Does the same person do all the work? Do family members take turns doing chores?

In the Miller family, Susan, the oldest daughter, ended up with all the chores. Her three younger brothers refused to help with dishes and cleaning. She either had to do more than her share or leave the house a mess. The situation improved when a social worker helped the family make a list of chores with work assignments for each member.

Now, at the end of each week, they have a family meeting to discuss the work sharing, and there is much less arguing. If someone is not doing the task to which he or she was assigned, it is discussed, and resentments are talked about and dealt with promptly.

Another trouble area is *time*. It is a good idea to set your curfew times down in writing:

> What time are you expected to be in the house in the evenings?
> Do you have a bedtime?
> What time are you expected home after school?
> Is there a reasonable limit to the amount of time any family member has a right to spend in the bathroom?

How late can you stay in bed on weekends and holidays without inconve-
niencing the others?

Arrange times that are suitable for your family.
When you all agree, post a schedule on the wall
where everyone can see it. Try to establish exactly
what is expected of you. This will make it easier
for you to know what your parents consider right
and what they think is wrong. If there are rules
that you disagree with, you should find the op-
portunity to discuss them with your parents.

Amy complained that her mother suggested a
weekend bedtime that was ridiculous. All her
friends stayed up much later. Amy felt that she
was a responsible kid. She certainly wasn't planning to stay up all night, as her mother feared.
With her understanding father, she talked to her
mother, and they came to an agreement which,
even though it was a compromise, satisfied everyone.

Planning, of course, will not solve all the problems. Rules change as you grow older or as cir-

cumstances change. However, if you stick to the agreed-upon schedules, there will be fewer arguments and less confusion.

If your parent continues to refuse to do anything about the drinking, your problems will continue even though you may understand them better. They will not just go away. Your home is different from the homes of most of the kids you know. You have been given some suggestions as to how to cope with these differences. Use the ideas that make sense for you and your family, don't worry about the ones that are not right for you. You will start to feel hopeful when changes for the better begin to happen.

4
Your "Other" Parent

You are not the only one in your household who is confused and unhappy. Your nonalcoholic parent is facing a lot of the same problems that you are. When you turn to that parent for help and understanding, remember that there will be times when he or she is upset, too, and will not be able to give you much comfort. Your nonalcoholic parent is probably angry and disappointed and has lots of worries. Some of those worries can be shared with you, but most of them have to be solved by your parent alone.

Each of your parents may try to make you

listen to complaints about the other. If they do, they are trying to involve you more than someone your age should be involved. You have a right to be your age, and that means that you should not be burdened with trying to solve the problems your parents have with each other.

One woman, married to an alcoholic man, thought that she could use her child to keep her husband from drinking. When her husband went out of the house, she worked it out so that their little girl would go with him. She thought he would be ashamed to drink when he had his child along. Of course, this "cure" didn't work, and it only made the child feel like a failure because she really couldn't stop her father from drinking. This frustrated mother hadn't been able to control her husband's drinking; she had succeeded only in making her child feel awful.

An eleven-year-old boy, Peter, was sent by his mother to a bar to bring his father home. Peter was terrified. Not only did he not want to go into the bar, the smell and noise of which he hated, but he was afraid his father would beat him up if he tried to get him to come home. Although he knew it wasn't the right thing to do, he hid in the bushes next to his house instead of going to get his father. When, two hours later, he saw his father stumble up the path to the house, he walked in after him. By the time he got in the door his parents had already begun an argument. Peter went to his room and turned on the radio—loud.

It is important that you not let your nonalcoholic parent involve you in a situation that will make you feel helpless. You can tell that parent that since you cannot do anything about the drinking problem, it is not fair to ask you to.

The people who are closest to the drinker are often the ones who have the most difficulty seeing what is going on. In Amy's family the kind of cereal that was eaten for breakfast was made an important issue. Each member of the family liked a different one. Amy liked Grape-Nuts; one sister wanted Froot Loops; another wanted Special K. Her father like Puffed Rice best. They argued about whether they should get out separate boxes of cereal each morning or whether they all should eat the same cereal and change to someone else's favorite on another morning. They got into tremendous fights about this unimportant issue because it allowed them to forget about the real problem—the drinking. It was really a kind of family defense system. But of course, the drinking issue was always lurking in the background.

When you hear your alcoholic father yell at your mother and she reacts by yelling at you, don't be surprised. A better way for her to handle her anger might be to cry or go for a walk. But when she takes it out on you, it is mostly because you are there and not because she doesn't love you. She is angry and frustrated and unhappy. She may also feel worthless and unloved. She expected a different kind of life, and she doesn't know what to do about what is happening.

It may actually seem to you that your mother is the cause of the discomfort and disorder in which you live. She may make you angry. She may be overly strict and make so many demands on you and your sisters and brothers that you begin to hate her for being unfair. Because she is so mean at times, it may even seem to you that your father prefers you to her. You may believe that if your mother were more loving, your father would not drink so much. In fact, you may hear him say, "If it weren't for your mother, I wouldn't be drinking." Possibly you agree with him. But remember, your mother has been put in the position of being the disciplinarian in your family. Your father probably doesn't care about details and just wants to be left alone. He may make up rules, but he can't be consistent about enforcing them. What seems important to him one day may be totally forgotten the next. When that happens, kids often just do whatever they want to do. So keeping order is up to your mother, and therefore, she may seem unnecessarily demanding.

It may be difficult, but try to understand how she feels. She bears most of the responsibility for the whole family. She tries to do her best, but she is constantly worried. Along with her worrying go fear and anger. If you react to her anger by getting mad at her, it is because you don't really understand how upset she is. Right now she is unable to act differently; she has trouble controlling her actions. You are going to have to wait and hope that the time will come when she will understand that the pressures she puts on the family and her overconcern for you are not helpful.

If it is your mother who drinks too much, your father may stay away from home a great deal. He may not come home when he is expected. As we have mentioned, it is not always the parent who drinks too much who disappoints the family. Many kids feel that when a father is away a lot, it is because he doesn't love his children. This is not so. You should understand that coming home may be painful for your father. There are many reasons to keep him away. The condition of the house may make him sad, or he may want to avoid arguments and hassles. He may feel that it is his fault that things have gotten out of hand, and he may deal with his guilt feelings by avoiding the situations which make him feel that way.

In addition, he has probably tried again and again to get your mother to stop drinking. He may feel that although he has done all in his power to change things, he has failed, and he feels hopeless.

On the other hand, your nonalcoholic parent may be tremendously concerned about what is going on and will react by spending as much time as possible helping the family. He or she will try to get the house in order and make things more comfortable. But trying to keep things quiet and avoiding fights take a lot of energy. So your "other" parent becomes moody, too.

You may wonder why, if there is so much fighting in your home, your nonalcoholic parent doesn't just move out. Why does he or she put up with the situation? Why don't your parents separate or get divorced? You may even be angry at them for staying together. Have you ever stopped to think that despite the drinking problem, your parents may still love each other?

To break up a home is frightening for anyone. As a grown person, has your mother ever lived without your father? There may be financial reasons for them to stay together. Raising a family takes a lot of strength and self-confidence. They may doubt their ability to do it alone. They may stay together hoping that the drinking will stop.

If your mother or father really did decide to leave, how would you feel? Most of the time you love your alcoholic parent even though he or she makes life extremely difficult for the family. In many ways it would be hard on either one of them to be alone.

Still, there are times when parents do have to separate. Your mother may still love your father, but she may be so unhappy with his drinking and the way he acts when he is drunk that she cannot live with him any longer. She doesn't want you to live with him either because she is worried about what might happen. Your father may feel the same way if it is your mother who is drinking.

One girl said that she blamed her mother for the fact that while drunk, her father hit her on the arm and gave her hideous bruises. She felt that her mother should have protected her, and the belief that she was uncared for was very up-setting.

If your father is the kind of alcoholic who becomes violent when he is drinking, he can harm you. Your mother may have decided to leave your father to protect you as well as herself.

It is also possible that your father or mother has been drinking so much for such a long time that they no longer love each other. The drinking has changed them, and they are not the same persons they used to be. You have seen them change.

How can you handle the hurt you feel, or will feel, should your parents decide to split up? If you allow yourself to feel that pain and accept the fact that you have been hurt, it will be easier to cope with it. If you hide your feelings from yourself and pretend that everything is OK, you will probably find it difficult to help yourself. In other words, you won't look for help if you don't think you need it or don't admit to yourself that you have a problem and are unhappy about it.

If you can build relationships with grown-ups

and kids outside your own family, you will get a feeling of independence and confidence in yourself. You will also be less affected by your parents' troubles even when they try to pull you into them.

Some parents get together again when the alcoholic partner stops drinking. There is very little point in your waiting for that time to come. Obviously there is no way of knowing when or if it will happen. The best thing for you is to go on with your own life and try not to let your parents' problems get in your way.

5
When Things
Get Really Bad

There are some extremely difficult situations that can occur when there is an alcoholic in the family. It is a good idea to be prepared for such problems, even though you probably will never be faced with them. The kinds of problems you may have to contend with will depend on how the alcoholic in your family behaves when he is under the influence of alcohol. For instance, if he is the kind of person who goes to sleep when he has had too much to drink, you won't have to worry about being beaten by him, but it would be realistic to worry about fires. Here are some of the situations about which you should think seriously.

DRINKING AND DRIVING

Riding in a car with a driver who is drunk is a very serious matter. There is every reason in the world to be scared when the driver swerves or reacts slowly to oncoming cars or has trouble seeing the road. In general, DO NOT DRIVE WITH ANYONE WHO HAS BEEN DRINKING! This may sometimes be a problem. How can you refuse to go along, for example, if it is a family outing or if there is no other possible way to travel? Think ahead! Discuss the matter with your "other" parent. Is there someone else who can do the driving? Have you an older brother or sister or grandparent or friend who drives? Are there alternative ways of getting to where you need to go? Is there public transportation in your community that will get you to your destination when there is no sober driver available? Taxis are expensive but sometimes necessary. Can you walk to where you are going? When there is no one to drive, can you stay overnight at the place you are visiting? Try to think of ways of getting places so that you do not have to depend on any driver who may have had too much to drink.

When a family trip or visit is planned, an agreement *ahead of time* about who will drive can often help avoid last-minute arguments. If you wait until the time has come to get into the car, a parent who has had too much to drink may not realize that he should not be driving and may insist on doing so. Then a scene which might have been avoided will follow. Try as hard as you can to avoid this kind of dangerous situation.

FIRE

Fire is another real hazard in homes where a parent drinks too much. Drinking and smoking often go together. If your parent smokes, the danger of fire is great because people who drink and smoke tend to get sleepy and drop their cigarettes. Then a couch or bed or chair can catch on fire easily. Do you know how to call the fire department and how to get out of your building in the event of fire? Is there a fire escape or an extra staircase or a rope route out of your home? If you are prepared for a serious situation, it becomes less dangerous and therefore less frightening. A basic rule if there is a fire: First get out of the house, and *then* call the fire department.

MEDICAL EMERGENCIES

Medical emergencies are common among people who have been drinking too much over many years. Such emergencies include vomiting blood, bleeding from the rectum, broken bones, having convulsions, or going into delirium tremens (DTs).

When the liver is scarred from long-term drinking, it doesn't function well and causes swelling of the blood vessels around the esophagus and stomach. These fragile vessels can burst and bleed heavily. Sometimes the blood is vomited up.

Blood also comes out in the stool. It has been partially digested by the time it comes out of the body, so blood coming from the rectum can range from bright red to maroon or even black. Another cause of bleeding is alcoholic gastritis —an inflammation of the wall of the stomach. The bleeding associated with gastritis is less severe. Although you should be concerned when you see blood, remember, a small amount of blood often looks like a lot.

Sometimes, by bumping into furniture or a wall, the alcoholic may be bruised badly enough to need medical treatment.

When a person who has been drinking heavily stops for a day or two, he occasionally develops convulsions. He may fall on the floor unconscious; his arms and legs will alternately shake and get stiff. In the process he can bite his tongue or lose control of his bladder.

Delirium tremens can occur if a person who is used to daily drinking has not been able to get alcohol for a few days. He becomes disoriented and doesn't know who or where he is. He may see and hear terrifying things that are purely imaginary. Symptoms of delirium tremens are usually accompanied by a high fever, nausea, shaking, and feelings of extreme anxiety.

If you find either one of your parents on the floor and you cannot awaken him or her, it is a medical emergency, and it is important to call for help. It is not always the drinking that is the only reason. Your sick parent may have taken an overdose of other medications along with the alcohol. It is common for alcoholics to use pills and alcohol in dangerous combinations. Another cause of passing out may be low blood sugar. But in any of these situations, medical attention is needed!

First call the doctor. If you don't know the name or can't find the phone number of a nearby doctor or your family doctor, then call an ambulance. It will come fast with paramedical people who have been trained to handle emergencies. Some communities do not have easy-to-call doctors and emergency facilities. Then call the police, who can bring help quickly for any sick person. Many communities have an emergency number that you can call.

If it is your mother who is unconscious, then

see if you can call your father. If it is your father who is ill, do you know where to reach your mother? If your sober parent is not available, is there a neighbor, relative, or friend whom you can call? Write down these important phone numbers, and leave them in a place where you can find them easily.

It is best to leave your parent where you find him. He feels sick and probably wants to be left alone. But you must try to get help. When your parent revives, he should be told what happened. It is possible that the fright he will feel at having passed out will get him to make a decision to stop drinking. Difficult as it may be for you, do not try to pretend that nothing happened. Your parent needs to know!

LOSS OF BLADDER CONTROL

Loss of bladder control is not an emergency, but it is a mess. A drunken person has little control over any function of his body. Urinating into his clothing is a common occurrence. It happens because the alcoholic has temporarily lost control of his body as a result of the action of the alcohol on the brain. Of course, it is unpleasant for everybody, and there is very little that can be done about it until the person with the drinking problem wants to do something about it himself.

SUICIDE

Suicide is much more common among alcoholics than it is in the general population. Sometimes parents who drink too much feel so discouraged and hopeless about themselves and their lives that they threaten suicide. These threats should not be ignored or kept secret; they should be taken seriously. If one of your parents talks about killing himself, you should always tell your "other" parent or someone who is close to your family. You will not be tattling. You will be trying to prevent a tragedy. People who make suicide threats are usually asking for help. It is important that you share your knowledge with someone who can help you help your parent.

BEATINGS

Some drinkers become rough and brutal when they have too much alcohol. You may have a parent who does exactly that. If you are beaten, hit, or knocked around by one of your parents, there are ways to protect yourself. Of course, you should first tell your "other" parent if you have one. However, he or she may be too frightened or upset to know what to do. And even when he or she wants to help you, that parent may have to go to family court to get an "order of protection." Usually, when the alcoholic sees a document from the court, he is likely to obey it. The nonalcoholic parent or you can then call the police at any time when threats are being made, and the police must remove the drunken person from the home.

If, for some reason, you don't want to or can't share this information with your "other" parent, you should tell another relative, a trusted neighbor, or a friend. Do not feel as if you are telling tales. You have a right to protect yourself.

Since it is hard for many people to believe that a parent beats his or her child, you may have to report the beating to someone whose job it is to handle such situations. Perhaps your teacher is a suitable person. Or there may be other school authorities who can help. They may call your parents into school and talk to them about how seriously their problems are affecting you. Or, they may refer them to a council on alcoholism or some other social service agency.

In some cases children have to be taken out of their homes, away from an alcoholic parent. They may have to live in a foster home for a period of time until the alcoholic does something about his drinking problem. When a child is taken away from a parent by the law, that parent often comes to realize the seriousness of his actions and goes for help for his alcoholism.

IMPROPER DRESS

While it is easy to talk about some problems, others are not often talked about openly. These relate to personal and sexual behavior. As you know, people who drink too much act in unusual and sometimes extraordinary ways. Since they are often unaware of their surroundings, they may not pay attention to the way they are dressed. They may be partially dressed, forget to close buttons and zippers, or they may be found walking around their homes without anything on at all. They may put on a shirt and not realize that they have forgotten their pants. If you have a parent whom you find undressed, the best thing for you to do is to tell that person to go get dressed or to finish dressing. You are surely embarrassed by a parent who doesn't take the care to clothe himself in an acceptable way. You may feel ashamed of him. If you can, let the alcoholic know, in words that are clear enough so that he can't mistake them, that you are upset by his sloppiness and that you don't like it.

SEXUAL ABUSE

A parent who is drinking too much may lose control of sexual impulses and may act in a way that could make you feel extremely uncomfortable.

You should not be sexually fondled, caressed, or forced to have intercourse or do anything that would be normal only between husband and wife (or two consenting adults). Intercourse with a member of your own family is incest, and it is illegal. You have a right to protect yourself by talking to the police, a doctor, or a school counselor. One of them will be able to help you out of your predicament. Since they are professional people, they will also keep your problem private.

One girl let her father's advances go on for so long that she eventually thought the only way out would be to kill either herself or her father. She was terrified that her mother would find out what was going on; she dared not tell the school authorities because she was afraid they would inform the police and she would then be treated as a criminal. To complicate matters, she also had good feelings about her father and didn't want anything to happen to him either. Finally, after unbelievable anguish, she gathered up the courage to talk to a doctor about her dilemma. He made arrangements to have her move out of her home to her aunt's house. That was a comfortable solution for her because she loved her aunt and uncle and cousins. He also arranged for her to talk to someone at a nearby mental health clinic. It took a long time, but eventually she was helped to come to terms with both her overpowering feeling of guilt and her resentment of having been used.

HOW TO GET IMMEDIATE HELP

If you need to get *help right away* and no one you know is available, there are places in your community where you can get immediate attention. In an emergency call the *police*. If the problem is a medical one—that is, if someone is in physical trouble (passed out, bleeding, beaten)—you should call the nearest hospital. If the help you are looking for is for yourself, you may ask for a "child abuse unit" or a "family crisis clinic." Most hospitals have these facilities. If the hospital you call doesn't have them, you may want to ask for the psychiatric department or the pediatric (children's) service. Many hospitals have "walk-in clinics," where help is immediately available.

If there is a *hot line* in your community, it will quickly help you reach the person who can help with your particular problem. The hot line people won't ask you for your name, and they will help you only over the phone; but they will know where you can call for more help. There may be a *council on alcoholism* (often listed under "Alcohol Information Center" in the phone book) in your community. Most towns have a telephone listing for Alcoholics Anonymous or Al-Anon. These agencies can be specifically helpful to people with alcoholism in their family.

In addition, there are many *social service agencies* where help is available:

> Family service agency
> Mental health association
> Youth service agency
> Youth consultation center
> Child guidance center
> Child guidance clinic

Children's bureau

Walk-in clinic (most often part of a hospital; sometimes a storefront)

Department of social services (listed under your county or state)

County agency (sometimes called Community Mental Health Board of Department of Mental Health Services)

Not all communities have all these resources. All communities have some of these resources. If you need help, be courageous—ask for it!

6
Holding Your Own

HIDDEN FEELINGS

John was exhausted. "I heard dishes being smashed all night, and this morning I found a mess of broken glass on the floor. I wish she'd croak!" John was talking about his mother to his teacher. A bus was taking the whole class on a museum trip. John had been the last to get on; the only seat left was next to his teacher, Mr. Gray. That was a stroke of luck. Mr. Gray noticed that John was moving slowly that morning and that he kept yawning. He finally asked him why he was so tired. John replied, "My folks kept me up all night making a racket. My dad had too much to drink, and my mom was giving him a hard time. She says she tries to control herself, but she bugs him so long that he finally starts cursing her out and throwing things . . . usually dishes . . . last night glasses." John yawned again.

Mr. Gray asked, "How come you manage to do such good work in school when all this stuff is going on at home?"

John answered, "The only way I can get my dad to pay any attention to me is to get good marks. If I could fly, he'd like that, too! School is a drag. It's tough to pay attention. My head is usually at home, wondering who's kicking whom and who's smashing things up."

It turned out that Mr. Gray knew something about the problem of alcoholism. He talked to John in a way that made John feel that he understood and didn't think less of him because of his problem. Most of the time John tried to hide his feelings, but this morning on the bus he could no longer cover up his fatigue or rid himself of his fears, or anger, or the feeling of shame he felt about his parents. It was a relief to talk to Mr. Gray.

As the bus traveled toward the museum, John started to feel some hope. Mr. Gray offered to call his parents and ask them to come to school so that he might speak to them. John wanted this, but he was worried, too. Mr. Gray's talking to his parents might just make them angry, and they might take it out on him. How many times had he been told not to talk about what went on at home? Once his parents had bribed him by promising him a new bike if he would just keep his mouth shut. Still, he figured that things couldn't get worse. He trusted Mr. Gray and hoped that with the teacher's support he might be able to talk to his parents about some of the painful things that troubled him. He might even get to the point of being able to tell them how ashamed he felt for them and how much he wished they would stop fighting, how much he hated his mother's complaints, how much he wanted attention from his father. Maybe his father would even help him put the broken basketball hoop back on the garage wall.

STOP PRETENDING—START TALKING

Maybe Mr. Gray could really help him change things. "Your parents' battles will probably continue," Mr. Gray told John. "But at least there is a chance that talking to them may make them more aware of the problem, and they then may try to get some help. In any case, if you keep burying your feelings, it will become harder to do anything about what troubles you. Talking about your worries will help separate your problems from theirs. It will help you see things more clearly. Stop pretending that drinking is not a problem. You know it is. You can talk to me; you can share some of your feelings with other kids, too . . . particularly if you go to an Alateen meeting [see Chapter VII] and find some new friends there. Those kids will understand from their own experiences what you're talking about."

After the museum trip Mr. Gray made arrangements to spend time alone with John each week for the rest of the school year. In their sessions together John was able to become more aware of the feelings that he had been bottling up inside for so long. He had been taking out his anger on smaller kids in school by beating them up and by picking on little kids who played on his street. He had also been stealing money from his father when he was drunk. Instead of helping him overcome his anger, this destructive behavior made him feel more and more guilty and upset with himself. Until Mr. Gray pointed it out to him, he couldn't see that he was harming himself. Mr. Gray and John continued to talk a lot about shame and guilt and blaming people. After a while John began to be able to look at his parents' problems more objectively and could refuse to take sides. He also came to realize that if he got off his parents' "merry-go-round," neither of them would have his support, and they would probably go for help sooner. By the end of the school year life seemed much brighter for John.

BRINGING FRIENDS HOME

One of the stickiest topics John talked about with Mr. Gray was about bringing friends home. Since he never knew whether or not his father would be there when he got home from school or whether or not he would be drunk, he worried a lot. He found that the best solution for him was *not* to bring friends home at all, and then he was sure that he wouldn't run the risk of being embarrassed.

If a friend does come home with you and you find that your mother, for example, has been drinking too much, you don't have to make explanations if your friend does not ask questions. Because you are used to the signs of drunkenness, there is a good chance that you will notice your mother's condition long before your friend does. Your friend may not even realize that your mother is drunk. On the other hand, if your friend does notice it, he or she may be more unnerved or frightened by it than you are simply because he or she is unfamiliar with drunken behavior. If an explanation is necessary, you know that your mother is sick, and you can say just that!

UNFAIR RESPONSIBILITIES

When you compare yourself to your friends, you may feel that not only are you not being taken care of but there is a great deal of extra work that you are required to do. You may be asked to take on responsibilities that ordinarily someone your age would not be asked to take on.

If your mother is drinking too much, you may be required to do the shopping and cooking. There are ways for you to cope. At a time when she is not drinking, try to speak to her. For instance, get together on a morning when she is feeling good. You may find that she is not interested in listening to you at all. And that will be that! But then, perhaps you can talk to your father about how you feel. He may be surprisingly helpful and understanding. After all, he and you share many of the same frustrations and disappointments.

If it is your father who is drinking too much and your mother expects you to take on his responsibilities, point out to her that while you can do some of these tasks, others may be too complicated for you to handle. There are some jobs, like fixing broken things or lifting heavy loads, that need to be done by someone with more strength and training than you have.

If you are the only child or the oldest child in your family, like Amy, you probably feel tired of many of the duties you have had to take on. Perhaps you have had to care for younger sisters and brothers because there are times when they really need your help and there is no one else who can dress them, feed them, or see that they get to the bathroom before they wet their pants. You may have had to wash them, watch them in the street, or take care of their general safety. One boy described how he was really being mother and father to his two younger sisters. He resented being put in this position, but he had no choice. His parents, both of whom were drinking heavily, were preoccupied and simply didn't take care of their kids.

If you do feel put-upon, there are times when you will have to say that you will not do so much work. Think carefully, and try to let your parents know that there are duties you cannot undertake.

If you are the youngest child in the family, there are many ways that you can help your older sisters and brothers with household chores. You can make life easier for everyone if you take care of your own clothes and bed. Certainly you are able to help with the kitchen work or with leaf raking or housecleaning or errands. Think of what you are best at; then do these things. At the same time do not forget about yourself. You need to have fun, too. There will be jobs that just won't get done!

If you live with a single parent and that parent is drinking too much, you may need someone from outside your home to help you take care of the household. Have you thought about who that person could be? Do you have a relative or a neighbor who might be a willing helper?

WAYS TO COPE

What should you do if you are yelled at for something you didn't do? Or maybe you did do something that at the time seemed perfectly all right. It is best *not* to talk back to a drunken parent. It can't help, and it will make you feel only worse about yourself. Wait until your parent is sober to make explanations.

Each family is different, and each alcoholic person reacts in a different, though characteristic, way to what he sees as annoyances. You can learn what to expect of the alcoholic in your family in certain situations. For instance, when John would walk out of the room while his father was yelling at him, his father would jump up and follow him, and there would be a fight. So John learned that he would do best to wait quietly. He knew that he was living with someone who was not thinking logically when he drank. Give your parent time to let his anger blow over. Ignoring his anger is close to impossible, but you can learn by experimentation the best way to cope with it.

Mr. Gray repeatedly told John, "When your parents argue, don't get involved in the problem! It's not yours! They may try to get you to take sides. They may ask you who you think is right. Don't try to make sense out of what could well be non-sense. Stay out of it! If you get involved, it will only make you feel worse and even more powerless. And you now know that when the action of the alcohol wears off, things will be different."

You do have a right to talk to your parents about your own needs. Timing your requests carefully takes planning and judgment. You will have to think twice when you want to talk about things that you know may cause explosions. Unfortunately, it is *you* who have to wait for the right moment.

IT'S OK TO BE ANGRY

Waiting for that right moment may make you angry. Some people have trouble even knowing when they are angry. The result is that they do things to themselves and to others without realizing why. Others have a hard time expressing their anger. Many people need professional help in order first to know that their anger exists and then to know how to handle it.

Young people handle anger in different ways. Some cry, kick the wall, or get into fights with their friends. Some sulk, slam doors, or shut themselves in their rooms. Some are mean to their pets. Others will go for long walks or bike rides. IT'S OK TO BE ANGRY, but you have to try not to use your anger in harmful ways as John did. He not only hurt himself by increasing his guilt, but hurt others, like the kids on the street he beat up.

If you know you are mad, you may want to say so to your parents. However, since you are in a special situation, it may be unwise or impossible to talk to them about how you feel. Then you will have to find someone outside your family to whom you can talk.

BUILD UP YOUR OWN WORLD

It may well be that, for now, your task is to take responsibility for your own life. You can enrich it with books, movies, friends, sports, music, and TV. Be in charge of your own life, and try not to concentrate on your parent's drinking problem.

Build up your own world! How well do you know your community? What is there to do after school in the afternoons or on weekends or during vacations? Are there after-school activities? For instance, are there sports or music? Are there clubs that are connected to school activities? Is there a recreation program in your neighborhood?

Is there a library near where you live? Is there a park? Are there safe places to ride a bike or to roller-skate? Is there a community program that may give you a chance to play after-school games, such as baseball, volleyball, football, or tennis? Do you live in a cold climate where there may be ice skating? Is there a community swimming program? Are there Scout troops or 4-H clubs? When you look, you may be surprised to find what your town or neighborhood has for kids to do.

If there is really nothing, you may want to start your own club or project. Try to find an adult who could be a leader or help you get things started.

What do other kids your age do when they are not in school? Do you have a friend with whom you like to spend time? Do you ever sleep overnight at your friend's home? Can you get permission from your parents to do so? For you an overnight party may be a way of getting some relief from the problems at home. For the time being you may have to settle for having fun at other people's homes.

If you don't or can't invite kids to your home, you may find that they are less likely to invite you. However, it will have nothing to do with kids not liking you. Some people will feel that if they are not invited to your house, they won't invite you to theirs. Again, you will have to put up with this kind of treatment. Keep in mind that you have gotten into this situation because there is a problem in your family that makes it impossible for you to invite people home.

Amy found that it was absolutely out of the question for her to have people over. Instead, she looked around for relatives to visit. Do you have aunts, uncles, cousins, or grandparents with whom you like to stay? Think about the possibilities. Ask your parents to help with plans for weekend visits and vacations away from home. If they help you make the arrangements, they will be more content with the decisions because you have made them together.

Amy also spent time with some older people who lived in a nearby retirement home. She found that many of them liked to have a young friend. She found as well that they took the place of her parents in some ways because they were interested in what she was doing and in how she was feeling. In addition, they enjoyed sharing their life experiences with her; this made her feel trusted and worthy of their respect and love.

PETS

Another decision you will have to make with your parents is about pets. They can be very comforting. They never judge you, and they're always glad to see you. However, discuss what kind of pet would be OK for you to have *before* you bring it home. Amy tells a sad story about the time she was given a kitten. When she brought it home, her parents wouldn't let her keep it. You can imagine how miserable and disappointed she felt. Her father told her that she could have a fish or a turtle instead; he knew they took less time to care for. This was a huge compromise for Amy, but she had to accept it.

WHOM CAN YOU TALK TO?

Everyone needs to have at least one person to whom he can talk about his problems. The person you share your feelings and concerns with should be someone you trust and preferably someone who can help you solve your particular problem. Even though you can cope with most of your family problems on your own, there are times when it is necessary to get help. A good idea is to identify helpers *before* you need them. Then you will know whom to go to if there is an emergency. John, of course, was lucky when he accidentally sat next to Mr. Gray on the bus. Although he might not have been conscious of searching for help, John was probably looking for someone with whom he could share his unhappiness.

Nowadays there are many people and agencies to help children when they are in serious trouble. The person who is probably easiest for you to contact is your school counselor, the guidance person, or perhaps your own teacher. Many schools have experts such as a psychologist, a guidance counselor, a social worker, or a nurse. These people are trained to talk to young people about special concerns. They can be both understanding and helpful.

But you may want to get help from outside school—from a family member or over the telephone or by going to see one of the people in an agency mentioned in Chapter V.

If you have an older brother or sister, one of them may be a good person to talk to. They certainly know the total family scene better than any outsider, and they often can be understanding and comforting, too. Or you may have a relative, such as an aunt, uncle, cousin, or grandparent, to whom you feel close enough to talk.

If there is no one in your family in whom you feel you want to confide, is there a neighbor you feel you can trust? Perhaps one of your friends has a mother or father whom you feel especially at home with. Or do you know a counselor from camp or someone from your church or synagogue? You don't have to belong to a church or synagogue in order to speak to the minister, priest, or rabbi.

Is there a doctor whom you like and who knows your family? He could be, but does not have to be, a psychiatrist. Or is your family in touch with a social worker or psychologist?

Because you probably feel ashamed, you may have decided that you will simply not talk to anyone about your home. You may feel that other people will feel sorry for you. Try not to let shame keep you from talking about what's going on. You are not talking to friends to get pity; you are talking to friends because sharing is comforting and because they may have the courage and wisdom to be able to help you. If you want to have the information that you share with others kept confidential, be sure to say so. You will run less of a risk of other people's learning about matters that you would prefer to keep private.

If you have a best friend whom you can totally trust, you are lucky! It takes everyone time to find a person in whom they can confide. John had known Mr. Gray for a whole year before he finally got to talk to him on the bus trip.

In looking for someone to whom you can talk about your problems, do not be surprised if many people don't understand. People who have never had any experience with alcoholism will find it difficult to believe some of the things you tell them. For instance, John once complained to a friend about the fact that his father drank all weekend every weekend. His friend couldn't believe him and thought he was making it up. Amy told a neighbor that her mother couldn't go to sleep at night without several drinks first. That neighbor just didn't understand as she had never known anyone who drank after dinner.

ALL FAMILIES HAVE PROBLEMS

The situation in your home is difficult to talk about. In a way, you want to protect your parents. After all, they are your parents, and most parents do their very best to give their children what they need and take good care of them. However, you may hear people talking in whispers about your alcoholic parent. This happens because people have trouble confronting the problems that go along with drinking, and they are ill at ease in talking about them directly. They may think that by whispering, they will spare you some of the pain. Sometimes they will hide from themselves the fact that you know very well—maybe better than anyone else—what is going on. They may think that because you are young, you don't know what is happening. They have trouble facing the facts about alcoholism. Facing the facts, of course, will make the sickness more understandable and also much less scary. The person who is sick can be helped more and sooner if people would not join in hiding the illness. One way to help a person with alcoholism is to let him know the consequences of the drinking.

It may be difficult for you to believe that other people your age have similar things happening in their homes. Young people can be cruel to one another and often say mean things. That doesn't mean that their own families are without troubles. Their troubles may be different from yours, but all families have problems—some more serious than others and some more easily solved than others. They may not talk about them either. They, too, may have learned not to trust anybody.

One of the most important facts for you to feel sure of and to know, down to the bottom of your heart, is that IT IS NOT YOUR FAULT that someone in your family drinks too much and has become an alcoholic. You are not to blame! You may think that when something bad happens to you, it is because of something bad you have done. You may even feel that you are being punished for bad thoughts or behavior. That is not so.

It doesn't matter how many times you have heard, "If it weren't for you, I wouldn't be drinking." Your alcoholic parent is looking for someone to blame, and you are an easy target. Even though you make your parent unhappy about some things you do, that does not mean that you have done anything worse than other kids do. You are not the cause of the drinking!

7
Alateen

If you are frustrated and confused by conditions in your home because you live with someone who drinks too much, you can get help from Alateen.

The Alateen groups were started in California in 1957 by a boy whose father was an alcoholic and who was helped by AA. His mother was in Al-Anon (a group meeting for relatives and close friends of alcoholics), so he patterned Alateen after it.

The main concern of Alateen kids is to help others who live with an alcoholic parent to learn about alcoholism and to help them cope with the problems it brings about. Not all their parents are still drinking. Some of them have been sober for months, some for years.

Today Alateen is made up of hundreds of groups of young people. By looking in the telephone book under AA or Al-Anon, you will be able to call someone who can tell you if there is an Alateen group in your community. If there is, you are in luck! Alateen groups usually meet once a week. Most members are teenagers, but often kids of eleven and twelve are included. They help one another by exchanging ideas and feelings. The help you can get from talking openly to people who understand what is going on in your home will amaze you. Once you have accepted the first step of Alateen, which is "the realization that you are powerless concerning your parent's drinking," you will be well on your way to understanding the problem.

What happens at an Alateen meeting? Alateen is like any club or group meeting that you may have attended at school, church, or synagogue. You will find most meetings take place in churches

—often in the basement or a room off the main part of the church. Some groups meet in a neighborhood clubroom. There is usually an adult leader who is a member of AA or Al-Anon and who will be there to start the meeting and to give it direction. That person is called a sponsor. However, most of the talking will be done by members of the group.

One boy talked about his mother who did most of the yelling even though his father was the alcoholic. This boy was angrier at his mother than at his father. He felt less guilty about his anger after another boy said to him, "I know exactly how you feel—I feel the same way." Another kid talked about how it felt to be at a party with a mother who was drinking too much and how ashamed he felt when she got drunk and acted silly and sexy. One girl said that her family moved so often that no sooner had she gotten to know her new neighborhood, than her parents packed up and went to a new place. She felt so resentful and angry that she vowed to herself that she wouldn't go with them the next time they moved. But this thought frightened her and made her feel more defeated and powerless. Her problems were partially solved when she discovered Alateen. Then, each time her parents moved, she was able to find an Alateen group, where she could feel comfortable even though she was in a new community.

One boy said that he went to Alateen just to get out of the house. Another boy said that he had gone to Alateen because his father had "dragged me there by the hair." He said he had felt mixed up and worried. His mother's denial of, and inability to see, her own trouble made him think she really didn't care—about herself or him or anyone. He was continually trying to get her to stop drinking. He kept saying things like, "Hey, Mom, I smell booze on your breath, and you're walking funny." His mother reacted by swearing at him and telling him that he should mind his own business. Each time he got up the courage to talk to her—one time about the empty bottles he found in his sister's dollhouse—she avoided the issue by asking him if he had cleaned up his room. He finally learned in Alateen that in no way was he going to be able to control his mother's drinking.

A twelve-year-old girl recalled an embarrassing experience with her mother. She told about the time her mother and she were driving home from a shopping trip. As soon as the car stopped at their home, and before they even had a chance to get out, her mother fell asleep in her seat behind the wheel. The girl couldn't awaken her mother, and she was embarrassed because she knew that the neighbors could see that she was sleeping in the parked car.

The discussions at Alateen can be about accidents . . . or a lost job . . . or a sleepless night. Any topic that worries a member of the group can be discussed. Some are heavy topics, and they can be frightening; but sometimes, too, they are unexpectedly funny. It is the sharing with others that makes Alateen so important to a lot of kids.

You will find that the meetings are relaxed and informal. You may sit on the floor. Or you may sit around a table. There is no special ceremony except perhaps a review of the aims and goals of Alateen.

In Alateen there are no assignments, no tests, no grades. No one will ask you to talk if you don't want to, but the more you contribute to the meeting by talking about yourself, the more meaningful it will be for you. You will feel better because you will have shared some of your loneliness, your confusion, and your helplessness.

If you know of no Alateen group near you, perhaps you would like to write for information about Alateen. If you write to Teen Secretary, Al-Anon Family Group Headquarters, Inc., Box 182, Madison Square Station, New York, N.Y. 10010, you will receive an answer very quickly in an unlabeled envelope. If there is no Alateen chapter near you, they will give you the address of their worldwide Meeting by Mail group. Then you will be able to write to and get letters from other people in similar straits.

Another alternative for you, if you find that there is no Alateen chapter near where you live, is to try to get one started. You can do that by calling or writing for information from an alcoholism information service (usually listed as such in the telephone book). Or you can call a number listed under Alcoholics Anonymous or Al-Anon Family Groups. They are equipped to help kids find a person who will know how to get an Alateen group going. In addition, a teacher or a guidance person or a youth advocate may be able to help you find the right person to get a group under way. Certainly there are others, like yourself, who need a place to go where they can talk about what is happening in their lives. And you might have to be the one to take the first step.

8
You and Alcohol

Do you look like your mother or your father? You may have been born with many of the same physical characteristics as your parents. For instance, if your mother has small feet, you may have small feet. If your father has blue eyes, perhaps you have blue eyes, too. Is your hair like your mother's or your father's? These physical traits are inherited and run in families. There are many studies under way attempting to determine whether or not there is an inherited factor that causes alcoholism.

Although we still do not know if alcoholism is

an inherited illness, we do know that if you have an alcoholic parent or close relative, such as an uncle, aunt, or grandparent, who is alcoholic, you are *more likely* to become alcoholic yourself.

A study of half siblings, brothers and sisters who have only one parent in common, showed some interesting results. In some cases studied the father of the oldest child was an alcoholic and the father of the youngest child was not. Both children were brought up by the same mother in the same home, but the child with the alcoholic father became an alcoholic in adulthood, whereas the younger child did not. However, as yet not enough research has been done to enable scientists to make final conclusions on whether or not alcoholism is inherited.

Another way that we get to resemble our parents is by watching them and imitating the way they do things. This process starts soon after we are born. Have you ever been told that you talk exactly like your mother or walk like your father? Your parents are the first models for your behavior. The behavior and mannerisms which you copy from them will probably stay with you for your entire life.

Studies show that if your father is an alcoholic, it is very possible that your mother has or had an alcoholic father. Girls who grow up in a home with alcoholic fathers often marry alcoholic men. They don't deliberately imitate their mothers, but they sometimes unwittingly tend to repeat the family pattern. Perhaps they identify with or want to become like their mothers. Or they search until they find men who remind them of the fathers they love. This, again, is a subject that needs more study. However, daughters of alcoholic men should be aware of this when it comes to choosing mates.

By watching their parents, young people learn to drink alcohol. One of your parents or perhaps both of them drink too much, so that when you are older, you, too, may drink too much. This sometimes happens even though you do not consciously want to imitate them. You may have decided that you are not going to drink as your parents do. You may not even like the taste of alcohol. However, since you have someone in your family who drinks too much, your chances of having a drinking problem are greater than if you came from a family where there was no alcoholism.

It is therefore natural for you to have fears about how it will be for you when and if you start to drink alcohol. Or if you have begun to drink, you may find that you are already having trouble with alcohol. Many children of alcoholics get into trouble as soon as they start drinking. They start getting drunk right away and mess up their lives. If you know the facts about alcohol, then if you drink, you can do so with caution. And remember, you always have the right to choose not to drink!

Since you may already have started to experiment with drinks, just to see how they taste or how they make you feel, it is important for you to keep in mind the fact that you will be making your own choices . . . over and over again. Unlike your alcoholic parent, you can still choose when you drink, how you drink, where you drink, with whom you drink, and if you drink at all.

You will want to make your decisions in the

light of what you know about alcohol and on the basis of what kind of life you want for yourself. Your decisions should not be based on what your friends do or on what you see on television or read in newspapers and magazines.

Magazines and newspaper ads for alcoholic beverages portray people as happy or rich or beautiful. The ads imply that they are that way because of the beer, wine, or whiskey they drink. If you stop to think, you will know that this is hardly the truth. You know that you will not get rich by sitting on a sailboat drinking beer. You will not become beautiful by sipping wine at a Swiss ski resort. You will not become happy by sitting in a club, drinking a certain kind of whiskey.

Your friends, too, may urge you to try drinking along with them. Or they may put pressure on you to take liquor from your parents' closet to "liven up" a party. So try to be conscious of what is being asked of you. You will want to make your own choices, not simply to succumb to ads or pressure from your friends.

Your decisions about drinking should be based on facts about alcohol. Alcohol is a colorless, odorless liquid. It has a bitter taste. Congeners, which are chemicals resulting from the manufacturing process, give each beverage its characteristic color, taste, and smell. Alcohol is a drug. It is not digested in the same way as other foods. Instead, it goes quickly through the walls of the mouth, throat, stomach, and small intestine and is then absorbed into the bloodstream. The blood carries it around the body and to the brain, where it acts on the central nervous system. Most of the alcohol a person drinks is metabolized (burned up) in the liver. The rest of it is excreted in the urine, through the skin, and in the breath. You have undoubtedly smelled the breath of a person who has been drinking. It has a characteristic or special smell. That person isn't necessarily an alcoholic. His body is simply getting rid of small amounts of alcohol which would otherwise come out in urine or perspiration.

If you have tried an alcoholic drink, you know how quickly you feel a change in your body or mind or, for that matter, in both. You don't have to wait long before you feel the effect of the alcohol. People have different reactions to it depending on their state of mind, how much they drink, how fast they drink, and whether or not they are accustomed to drinking. In a social situation people usually feel more talkative and friendly. When people drink alone, they are more apt to feel sad and tend to go to sleep.

To make a generalization about how you will feel when you drink a lot is difficult because each person has a different physical makeup and therefore reacts differently to drugs. The most common reaction to being drunk or intoxicated is first to feel happy and then to get numb, glassy-eyed, or sleepy. You may begin to burp or get hiccups, particularly if you drink bubbly drinks. Then your speech gets thick or slurred, your judgment is impaired, you have memory lapses, and your physical coordination starts to go. You may stagger when you walk and sometimes may even fall down. If you continue drinking, you will eventually pass out or go to sleep. Or if you drink too much too fast, you will become dizzy, nauseated, and confused and may lapse quickly into a coma. And sudden death may occur. This can happen when the central nervous system is depressed to such a degree that the physical body functions cannot continue.

As far as scientists know now, alcohol does no harm to the body when it is taken in small amounts. One thing they caution pregnant women about, however, is that alcohol, even in small amounts, may increase the chance of giving birth to an abnormal baby. Harm most certainly results to anyone when alcohol is taken in large amounts over a long period of time. Therefore, social drinkers get into trouble with alcohol only on the occasions when they drink too much at a time and get drunk and say and do things that they would ordinarily not say or do.

Noah, a high school student, did not realize that there was any difference in the alcoholic strength of vodka and beer. He thought that a glass of beer had the same amount of alcohol as the same size glass of vodka. One day he was with his friends who were drinking beer. He hated the taste of beer but didn't mind vodka, which is nearly tasteless. So, as his friends drank their glasses of beer, he gulped his full glass of vodka. Within minutes he went into a coma and ended up in the hospital. Luckily the boys with whom he was drinking got him to the hospital quickly and knew that he'd been drinking so they could tell the admitting doctor in the emergency room what had happened. Not all drinking stories end up as happily as this one. Many kids die each year as a result of chugalugging drinks about which they know nothing.

It is important to know that the content of drinks, in terms of alcohol, is different. Beer is 5 percent alcohol; wine is about 12 percent alcohol, and hard liquor or distilled spirits (rye, scotch, gin, vodka) is usually about 40 percent alcohol (or 80 proof). A can of beer, a glass of wine, or a shot glass (one and a half ounces) of whiskey all contain the same amount of alcohol. So, in drinking a glass of vodka, Noah drank about eight times as much alcohol as his friends each of whom had a can of beer. If he had taken the vodka very slowly during the course of the evening, he would have gotten high, but he would not have become unconscious and ended up as he did.

Two girls passed out at a junior high school dance after slugging straight whiskey. They didn't know the facts. They thought that "a drink is a drink." They didn't realize what gulping down a drink could do to them. They, too, were hospitalized.

Because of our tax laws and the way our legal alcoholic beverage controls are written by the government, companies that produce bottled or canned beer are not required to indicate the amount of alcohol on the outside of the container. But just because the cans aren't marked, and in spite of what people like to think and say, beer has alcohol in it!

Alcohol is a food. It has calories. They are called "empty calories" because the alcohol has no nourishing qualities such as vitamins or minerals. A glass of wine has about 120 calories, a glass of whiskey has about 125 calories, and a can of beer has about 150 calories. So people who are watching their weight should watch their drinking, too.

Here are some facts to know when and if you decide to drink:

- Get to know how *your* body reacts to alcohol. Everyone has different reactions. For instance, women react to alcohol in relationship to where they are in their menstrual cycle. During premenstrual days a smaller amount will make them drunker than at other times of the month. Do not let alcohol surprise you.

- If you drink, eat *first*. Also, eat while you are drinking.

- Always sip your drinks slowly. Then the alcohol will reach your brain slowly so that you will not have side effects, such as dizziness or vomiting. Chugalugging or gulping alcohol to show that you can drink faster than others is a dangerous way to drink. Do not try to get into that kind of competition.

- If you are thirsty, drink water or sodas. (They are cheaper.) Then you will not be tempted to gulp alcoholic drinks.

- Alcohol should not be combined with any kind of drug (including aspirin).

- Drinking to cover up sadness, to make yourself feel better, or to solve problems will work for only short periods of time. Eventually you will have to deal with the problem itself.

- Drinking when you are trying to do something that requires you to be alert or responsible will result in your failing at whatever you are trying to do. Drinking while you are baby-sitting or riding a bike is totally irresponsible.

- If you drink just to drink or just to get drunk, you are not acting responsibly. If you do drink, it should be done along

with other activities and not be an end in
itself.

- You do not have to drink to please friends.
  You do not have to give in to social
  pressure in order to have friends. In fact,
  your friends may respect you more if
  you stick to your own convictions. You
  do not have to drink because others are
  drinking.

- Sneaking drinks will result only in making
  you feel sick. It will also make you feel
  guilty.

- The only way to sober up if you have had
  too much to drink is to let time go by.
  A general rule is that it will take as many
  hours as the number of drinks you've had
  to recover from the effects of alcohol. Black
  coffee, cold showers, or running around
  in circles will not speed up or change this
  rate of recovery.

Here is a checklist* for you to decide for yourself if alcohol is becoming a problem for you:

1. Are you ever absent from school because of drinking?
2. Do you need a drink to make you feel better around other people?
3. Do you ever hide your beer, liquor, or wine?
4. Do you feel braver when you drink, less afraid?
5. Do you ever drink alone?
6. Do you drink as a way to stop worrying?
7. Do you feel guilty about your drinking?
8. Do you get upset when anyone says you drink too much?
9. Is it necessary for you to drink in order to have fun?
10. Does drinking make you feel equal to other kids?

* From *Kids and Drinking* by Anne Snyder, copyright © 1977 by Anne Snyder, published by CompCare Publications, Minneapolis, Minn.; reprinted by permission.

11. Do you sneak drinks from your parents' supply or anyone else's?

12. Did you ever steal money to buy beer, liquor, or wine? Did you ever pay someone to buy it for you?

13. Did you ever steal beer, liquor, or wine?

14. Have you stayed away from the "straight" kids since you started drinking?

15. Do you mostly hang around with kids who drink?

16. Do most of your friends drink less than you do?

17. Do you drink until you are drunk or until the bottle is empty?

18. Have you ever forgotten what happened while you were drinking?

19. Have you ever been arrested or had any medical treatment because of drinking?

20. Do you think you have a drinking problem?

A "yes" to one question is a warning.

A "yes" to two questions, chances are you are getting into trouble with alcohol.

A "yes" to three questions or more means that alcohol has almost certainly become a serious problem for you.

THE FUTURE

As has been mentioned, there is still much that is not known about why people drink too much and become alcoholic. The answer may be a psychological one. Why do people need chemical relief from stress? Or it may be physiological. Is there something in the human body that tends to make some people drink more than others? Or does the problem have a social source? Why do people in some societies have different drinking patterns from people in others? These questions have been answered only in part. The complete answers are still a matter of the future. What we do know is that one can stop drinking. Thousands of people do. They get well and lead happy lives together with their families.

You live with at least one parent who drinks too much. When you have faced that fact and learned something about alcoholism, your hardships and anxieties will be more understandable. You know where to get help and that there are ways of dealing with your situation in order to make it easier. You know that you are not alone. Go to an open meeting of AA; it will give you hope. You don't have to feel guilty about your family because you have done nothing to hurt them. You have some "tools" that you can use in order to improve your life. Nothing will change if you don't change it. You will need courage, and you will need patience. But you have made a start.